IN
MY TOWN

IN
MY TOWN

with illustrations by
Richard Scarry

gb. Golden Press • New York
Western Publishing Company, Inc.
Racine, Wisconsin

In My Town

A town is a small city.
Can you count the buildings
in my town? Do you see
a statue somewhere?

Do you see:

a church
a bridge
a house with a green roof

Beep! Beep! Here comes the town bus. Can you count the passengers? How many are there? I wonder where they are all going.

Do you think they are going shopping?

At the Store

We can buy almost anything at the store.

At the grocery store,
we can buy food.

There is a store for
eyeglasses and sunglasses.

Father Cat is trying
on some hats at the hat
store. Do you think that
one is the right size?

Kitty and Babykins like to go to the
toy store with Grandma. She always buys
them a present. Which toy would you choose?

Daddy Bunny is shopping at the hardware
store. Do you see a stove? a lawnmower?
a rake? a broom? a tractor? a wheelbarrow?

Doodledoo has some fine new shoes
from the shoe store.

Ma Pig shops at the butcher shop for meat.
Hey, what's going on? That butcher can't
see what he's doing!

Tom Cat found his new tuba at the music store.

And look at those fancy beggars!
They've been to the clothes store. They
all have new suits. Don't they look fine!

At the Garage

Sometimes a car stops working.
Then the car has to go to the
garage for repairs. Do you see
Mr. Fixit Fox? He is the repairman.
He certainly has a lot of work to do.

When Dingo's car broke down,
he took it to Mr. Fixit Fox for repairs.
Mr. Fixit Fox and his helper Chips
Beaver went right to work. Do
you think they can fix Dingo's car?

Point to:

hammer
saw
tire
garage
gas pump
tow truck

In the City

Do you see:

bus
fire engine
motorcycle
sidewalk cafe
mail truck
apple cart
Dingo

Oh, look out! Here comes Dingo, driving
through the city streets. Where could he
be going in such a hurry?

What confusion! The mail truck hits the
fire truck. The bus just manages to stop
in time. There are apples everywhere. When
will that Dingo learn to drive more carefully?

The Barber Shop

Ma Pig takes her piglets to the barber shop for a haircut. Why are those silly piglets crying? A haircut doesn't hurt. Do you cry when you get a haircut?

A Restaurant

Dingo goes to a restaurant for dinner when he doesn't want to eat at home. I really think he should leave his car in the parking lot, don't you?

The Doctor's Office

We go to the doctor's office for a check-up.
Look—there is Doctor Pill having a check-up
himself. Nurse Nora says Doctor Pill is fine.
Now he is getting a shot to help him stay healthy.

The Library

At the library,
we can borrow a
book to take home
and read.

QUIET PLEASE

At School

Things We Do at School

We learn to read.

We learn to write.

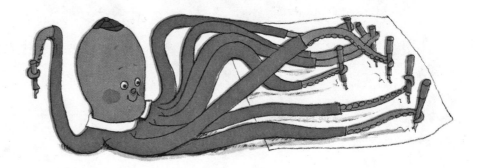

We learn how to measure things.
Can you tell ... how long is Squigley?

Things We Should Not Do at School

The teacher does not look happy. Can you tell why? Where is a better place to throw a paper airplane?

Why are these bunnies fighting in school? They don't want to share their crayons. The teachers will help them learn to share. Do you share your toys?

At the Park

There are lots of things to do at the park.

Do you see someone:

sleeping in the shade
playing tag
making mud pies
fighting
sliding
riding a bicycle
playing catch

At the Train Station

Beep, beep...look out, Beggars! Here comes Dingo, over the bridge to the train station. Why is he in such a hurry?

Oh, I see. Dingo was in a hurry to catch
a train. Most people leave their cars behind,
but not Dingo. Good, he is getting a ticket.
Now maybe he will learn to drive more carefully.

Do You Have One in Your Town?

a swimming pool?

a fountain?

a crosswalk?

a hot dog stand?

a castle?

a cheese store?

an upside-down house?